KU-271-321

# HARRY POTTER

# The Ultimate Quiz Book

Unofficial and Unauthorised

## Jack Goldstein

Copyright © Jack Goldstein 2012

All rights reserved

No part of this publication may be reproduced, stored in a retrieval system, or transmitted in any form or by any means, without the prior permission in writing of the publisher, nor be otherwise circulated in any form of binding or cover other than that in which it is published and without a similar condition including this condition being imposed on the subsequent publisher.

This book benefits from fair use provisions as set out in applicable copyright and trademark law. All characters and relevant information from within the world of Harry Potter are the intellectual property of J.K. Rowling, to whom all of us are indebted to for bringing us such a wonderful and magical world.

First published worldwide by

Andrews UK Limited
The Hat Factory
Bute Street
Luton
LU1 2EY

www.andrewsuk.com

ISBN 978-1-78166-242-7

# Contents

*To my family and friends*

# HARRY POTTER
## The Ultimate Quiz Book

# Introduction

The magical world of Harry Potter and his friends (and enemies!) is one that is now host to a wealth of wonderful information. Over seven books, J K Rowling has introduced us to a fantastical place where I am sure many of us would like to live – despite the risks of coming across Dark Wizards or scary beasts!

This quiz aims to add one more bit of fun to that world, by testing the reader's knowledge. These questions are based on the world as told to us in the books, rather than the series of films – as the two are sometimes quite different!

Perhaps you will read this book on the bus home after a long day at work or school, or maybe you will test your friends to see if they are as much of a magical expert as you are. Whichever way you use these pages, I hope you enjoy reading them as much as I did whilst writing them!

Good luck with the quiz!

*Jack Goldstein*

*September 2012*

# The Questions

# Harry – Part 1

1. When is Harry's birthday?

2. Where does Harry live?

3. Who brought Harry to the Dursleys' as a baby?

4. What is the shape of the Scar on Harry's head?

5. What did Harry talk to at the zoo?

6. What was Harry's father's first name?

7. And his mother's?

8. What special gift did Harry get on his first Christmas morning at Hogwarts?

9. What animal is produced by Harry's Patronus spell?

10. Who did Harry share his first kiss with?

# Hermione – Part 1

11.  What is Hermione's middle name?

12.  What animal is Hermione's Patronus?

13.  Who does Hermione attend the Yule Ball with?

14.  What device did Hermione using to fit in her extra classes?

15.  What is the name of Hermione's pet cat?

16.  What effect did the Densaugeo spell have on Hermione?

17.  In which subject did Hermione not get an Outstanding grade O.W.L.?

18.  What spell does Hermione use on Neville in the first book?

19.  What profession are both Hermione's parents?

20.  In which month is Hermione's birthday?

# Ron – Part 1

21. What colour is Ron's hair?

22. What is Ron's middle name?

23. How many siblings does Ron have?

24. What does Ron get from his mum after using the flying car to get to school?

25. What did Ron buy Harry for his 13th birthday?

26. What did Ron try to repair his wand with?

27. Which character does Ron play in the game of chess in the first book?

28. True or false: Ron is pure-blood?

29. Which animal is Ron most scared of?

30. What Quidditch position does Ron play?

# Hogwarts – Part 1

31. What does the Hogwarts motto "Draco Dormiens Nunquam Titillandus" mean?

32. What decides which houses the students will go into?

33. What colour is the Slytherin banner?

34. Who - or what - is Peeves?

35. What are the creatures that pull the Hogwarts carriages called?

36. What is the password to the Griffindor common room in Harry's first year?

37. Which four animals are on the Hogwarts coat of arms?

38. In Harry's first year at Hogwarts, whose name is the first to be called out to be sorted?

39. How many items are there on Mr Filch's list of forbidden objects?

40. What is the password to open the prefects' bathroom?

# The Wizarding World – Part 1

41. What are the three different forms of wizarding currency?

42. Who guards the wizarding prison of Azkaban?

43. What is the name of the wizard's hospital?

44. Who greets you at reception there?

45. And who founded it?

46. What is the name of the wizard high court of law?

47. Name the main wizarding newspaper?

48. What is the name of the all wizard village children can visit (with permission from their parents)?

49. And what do the Harry, Ron and Hermione buy to drink there?

50. From what material is a Remembrall made?

# Beasts and Animals – Part 1

51.    What is Fluffy guarding in the first book?

52.    And what puts Fluffy to sleep?

53.    What is the name of Neville's toad?

54.    What is the name of the Weasley family's owl?

55.    What is the name of the Hippogriff in the third book?

56.    And when he is given a new name, what is it?

57.    What sort of dog is Fang?

58.    What creature is hiding in the Chamber of Secrets?

59.    The blood of which creature kept Lord Voldemort alive in the first book?

60.    And at what age does this creature grow its horns?

# Quidditch – Part 1

61.  What are the three balls used in Quidditch called?

62.  How many points is it worth to catch the smallest ball?

63.  How many players are in a Quidditch team?

64.  What are the playing positions in Quidditch?

65.  Who are Ron's favourite Quidditch team?

66.  What type of broomstick is Harry given in the first book?

67.  Who is captain of the Gryffindor Quidditch team when Harry joins Hogwarts?

68.  Who was responsible for the rogue Bludger in the second book?

69.  Who was the captain of Slytherin's Quidditch team in Harry's first year?

70.  How many Quidditch fouls are there?

# Spells and Potions – Part 1

71. What is the name for the language used when talking to snakes?

72. What is the incantation for the levitation spell?

73. Which spell would you use to disarm an opponent?

74. How many unforgiveable curses are there?

75. And can you name them?

76. Which is the worst of these, and what is it known as?

77. What spell is used to open doors?

78. Which word lights up a wand?

79. What is the spell to repel a Boggart?

80. What words are used to produce a Patronus Charm?

# Other Characters – Part 1

81. Who is the headmaster at Hogwarts in Harry's first year?

82. What are He Who Must Not Be Named's supporters called?

83. Who runs The Three Broomsticks?

84. Who is the conductor on the Knight Bus?

85. And who is the driver?

86. Who was the creator of the Philosopher's Stone?

87. Who is the commentator at Hogwarts for the Quidditch matches?

88. What's the name of Colin Creevey's brother?

89. What is the name of Sirius Black's younger brother?

90. Who was killed by a forbidden curse instead of Harry?

# Books and the Like – Part 1

91. What colour are howlers?

92. Rita Skeeter is a reporter for which newspaper?

93. Where did Hermione read about the ceiling at Hogwarts?

94. And who wrote it?

95. What must you do to the Monster Book of Monsters to open it?

96. Which magazine test rides all new broomsticks?

97. What is the name of the wizard magazine?

98. What award did 'Witch Weekly' give Gilderoy Lockhart?

99. Who wrote A History of Magic?

100. Harry borrowed a copy of Advanced Potion Making; who did it belong to previously?

# The Weasley Family – Part 1

101. What are Mr & Mrs Weasley's first names?

102. Which of the Weasleys is taken into the Chamber of Secrets?

103. What is the make and model of the flying car?

104. What is the name of the house where the Weasleys live?

105. And how many hands does the Weasley family's clock there have?

106. Who does Ginny date before Harry?

107. What do Fred and George use to listen into conversations?

108. Which member of the Weasley family has a pony-tail and an earring?

109. And who is he engaged to?

110. In which department was Mr Weasley found after being attacked?

# Hogwarts Teachers – Part 1

111. Who teaches Charms?

112. Who teaches Transfiguration?

113. And how long has he or she been at Hogwarts?

114. What animal can he or she turn into?

115. Who teaches History of Magic?

116. What is Professor Lupin's secret?

117. What is Professor Sprout's first name?

118. Who was headmaster when Tom Riddle was at Hogwarts?

119. Who taught "Care of Magical Creatures" before Hagrid?

120. What secret did Harry discover about Filch which might explain his grumpy demeanour?

# General Knowledge – Part 1

121. Which plant likes to wrap itself around its victims?

122. What language do Merpeople speak?

123. To which local comprehensive school was Harry due to go?

124. How did Sirius Black escape from prison?

125. And what name do the trio refer to him as?

126. What part of you is hidden in a Horcrux?

127. Which sickly-sweet (by appearance, anyway!) teacher became the new Defence Against the Dark Arts teacher in the fifth book?

128. Which family does Dobby serve?

129. What colour is the knight bus?

130. In which English county does Nicolas Flamel live?

# Shops

131. Where did Harry buy his wand?

132. How many galleons does it cost?

133. Who owns the ice cream parlour in Diagon Alley?

134. What are the names of the two pubs in Hogsmeade?

135. What is the name of Fred and George's business in the later books?

136. And what is its address?

137. What does Madam Malkin sell?

138. What is the name of the main sweet shop in Hogsmeade?

139. Where would you go in Diagon Alley to buy a pet?

140. How much does it cost for a course of apparition lessons?

# Dumbledore

141. What bird does Professor Dumbledore keep as a pet?

142. And What item does it bring to Harry in the Chamber of Secrets

143. What has a cockroach cluster got to do with Dumbledore?

144. What mysterious magical items are Harry and Dumbledore trying to find in the latter books?

145. And how many does Dumbledore believe there are?

146. Where does Dumbledore store his excess memories?

147. Which wizard did Dumbledore defeat in 1945?

148. What stuffed creature was atop the witch's hat that came out of the cracker Dumbledore and Snape pulled?

149. Professor Dumbledore has a scar above his left knee in the shape of what?

150. How many uses of Dragon Blood did Dumbledore discover?

# He Who Must Not Be Named

151. What is His name (after he changed it)?

152. What is the name of His snake?

153. True or false: He is pure-blood?

154. How many brothers did He have?

155. What is the length of His wand?

156. Who paid for Him to attend Hogwarts?

157. Who did He go to work for when he left Hogwarts?

158. How much did His mother sell a particular locket for?

159. What three things do Harry and Him have in common?

160. What is the name of the village where the Riddles lived?

# Hagrid

161. What did Hagrid give Harry for Christmas in the first book?

162. And what was his official job title at the time?

163. Where does Hagrid keep his wand?

164. What was the name of Hagrid's Dragon?

165. And what type of Dragon is he?

166. What did Hagrid give to Harry for his thirteenth birthday?

167. Who does Hagrid believe is also a half-giant?

168. Which of Hagrid's Parents was a Giant?

169. And what was he or she called?

170. What is the name of the Giant that Hagrid brings back with him from a trip away from Hogwarts?

# Harry – Part 2

171. What was the number of Harry's room at the Leaky Cauldron?

172. What interesting item did Harry find after his night visit to the library the first Christmas that he was at Hogwarts?

173. Who did Harry meet in The Leaky Cauldron before the start of his first year at Hogwarts?

174. Who looked after Harry when the Dursleys went out?

175. What was Harry's mother's maiden name?

176. What creature's feathers do Harry and Lord Voldemort have as part of their wands?

177. What does the scar on the back of Harry's hand say?

178. Which wood is Harry's wand made of?

179. Which wood was his father's wand made from?

180. Which career does Harry want to have?

# Hermione – Part 2

181.  What does S.P.E.W stand for?

182.  And how much does it cost to join?

183.  What did Hermione Knit in relation to this?

184.  On the subject of abbreviations, what does DA stand for?

185.  And what does Hermione give to every member?

186.  What Spell did Hermione cast on a student during the Quidditch trials?

187.  And on whom did she cast it?

188.  Whose party did she then take him to?

189.  What exam clashes with Hermione's Ancient Runes one?

190.  Who is Hermione married to at the end of the final book?

# Ron – Part 2

191. Who does Ron ask for an autograph in the fourth book?

192. When Ron gets a new wand in the third book, what is it made of?

193. And How Long was it?

194. Who gave Pigwidgeon to Ron following the loss of Scabbers?

195. And who actually named it?

196. What does Dumbledore bequeath Ron in his will?

197. What did Harry buy Ron for his 17th birthday?

198. What did Ron eat that contained a love potion?

199. On the subject of girls, who did Ron date, kiss and break up with?

200. When Ron was poisoned what did Harry use to save him?

# Hogwarts – Part 2

201. Who haunts the girls' toilets on the first floor?

202. How many secret passages lead from Hogwarts to Hogsmeade?

203. Who usually guards the entrance to the Gryffindor Tower?

204. What are O.W.L.s?

205. What is the place that Dumbledore's Army practice in called?

206. How many schools take part in the Triwizard Tournament?

207. Name them!

208. And what is the minimum age for a competitor?

209. What does the flying car crash into at Hogwarts

210. What was Quirrell trying to get out of the mirror in the first book?

# Beasts and Animals – Part 2

211. What got into the castle on Halloween night of Harry's first term?

212. What type of owl is Hedwig?

213. What kind of creature is Aragog?

214. And who attended his funeral?

215. What did Professor Slughorn want from Aragog's body?

216. Where is Kreacher sent to work?

217. Name the centaur who helped Harry in the forbidden forest?

218. Which animal represents 'The Grim'?

219. What is Sirius's house-elf called?

220. On what does Professor Moody demonstrate the Imperius Curse?

# Quidditch – Part 2

221. Who was the only girl on the Ravenclaw Quidditch team?

222. Who insists that Harry and his friends support the Ireland Quidditch Team at the world cup?

223. And who did Ireland beat in the Semi Final?

224. Who did they play in the final?

225. And which of these two won?

226. Who refereed the final?

227. How much were a pair of Omniculars at the World Cup?

228. Which type of wood is the handle of a Nimbus 2000 made from?

229. Who banned Harry from playing Quidditch in his fifth year?

230. What make of broom does Harry get in his third year?

# Spells and Potions – Part 2

231. Which spell reveals the last spell a wand performed?

232. Harry, Ron and Hermione make which special potion in the second book to fool Malfoy?

233. What is Mandrake Root used for?

234. Which potion does Professor Lupin take regularly?

235. What is Felix Felicis?

236. And how long does it take to prepare?

237. Which plant did Harry use during one of the Triwizard challenges?

238. What happens when someone takes the potion Veritaserum?

239. The pus from which plant is a powerful cure for acne?

240. And what does that plant look like?

# Other Characters – Part 2

241. Which animal can Rita Skeeter turn into?

242. What is Fleur Delacour's sister called?

243. Who does Tonks fall in love with?

244. Who edits the Quibbler?

245. Who is the landlord of The Leaky Cauldron?

246. What does Nearly Headless Nick celebrate each year to which Harry and his friends are invited?

247. Into which Hogwarts house was Owen Cauldwell sorted?

248. What are the first names of Sirius's evil cousins?

249. Who replaced Cornelius Fudge as Minister of Magic?

250. Who accidentally opens a parcel with a cursed necklace in it?

# The Weasley Family – Part 2

251. What magical item do the Weasley twins give to Harry in his third year?

252. What is Mr Weasley's nickname for his wife?

253. How many Galleons was Mr Weasley fined for bewitching a car?

254. What does Mrs Weasley give Harry for supper when he arrives at the Burrow before starting his Sixth year at Hogwarts?

255. Who is Percy Weasley's boss?

256. And what does he call Percy?

257. How many O.W.L.S. did Percy take?

258. What is the name of Percy's (actual) Owl?

259. What department is Mr Weasley the head of?

260. How many Galleons were in the Weasleys' vault at Gringotts?

# The Dursleys

261. What is the name of Uncle Vernon's company?

262. How many presents did Dudley get for his birthday in the first book?

263. What do Dudley's gang call him?

264. And what does Aunt Petunia call him?

265. What school do the Dursleys say Harry goes to?

266. How many dogs does Aunt Marge have in total?

267. And which department was sent to deflate her?

268. What colour were the tailcoats worn at Smeltings School?

269. Which one of the Dursleys throws ornaments at Mr Weasley?

270. To which hotel did Uncle Vernon take his family and Harry to escape Harry's initial letters from Hogwarts?

# Harry – Part 3

271. Who tied Harry to a gravestone?

272. What extra subject did Harry take with Snape?

273. From which wood was Harry's mother's wand made from?

274. Which three major items did Harry inherit from Sirius?

275. Who did Harry take to Slughorn's party?

276. Which street does Harry end up in the first time he travels by Floo Powder?

277. Who did Harry duel with at the "duelling club"?

278. Which ghost did Harry meet when he was in the lake?

279. What was the name of the road on which Harry first saw the knight bus?

280. And when he gets on, what name does Harry give Stan instead of his own?

# Hogwarts Teachers – Part 2

281. What is Professor Flitwick's first name?

282. What role does Professor Tofty have?

283. Which potions teacher returns to Hogwarts after a long absence?

284. Professor Grubby-Plank took over from which teacher?

285. Who is the new Divination professor in Harry's final years?

286. What is Madame Pomfrey's first name?

287. Which dashing wizard becomes the Defence Against the Dark Arts Teacher in Harry's second year?

288. Who is the head of Hufflepuff House?

289. Professor Sinistra teaches in which department at Hogwarts?

290. Who brought Colin Creevey to Madam Pomfrey?

# General Knowledge – Part 2

291. What are N.E.W.T.S?

292. To where does the tunnel under the Whomping Willow lead?

293. Professor Trelawney's prophecy could apply to who else?

294. Who are Moony, Wormtail, Padfoot and Prongs better known as (make sure you get the correct order)?

295. Which member of the Order of the Phoenix is working for the muggle prime minister?

296. Who comes to Harry's rescue when he's hiding from Professor Lupin (in werewolf form)?

297. Which competitor wants to return to England to improve her language skills?

298. From which vault did Hagrid take something from at Gringotts?

299. Name the Gryffindor ghost's full name

300. And how many times was he hit in the neck with a blunt axe?

# Books and the Like – Part 2

301. Which book does Dumbledore bequeath to Hermione?

302. How many Galleons formed the prize money in the Daily Prophet Prize Galleon draw?

303. What did Harry use to keep the Monster Book of Monsters shut?

304. What name got inscribed on Ron's 'Advanced Potion Making' Book

305. Who is the author of 'Advanced Potion Making'?

306. Who wants to write Harry Potter's biography?

307. How did people who had read 'Sonnets of a Sorcerer' speak for the rest of their lives?

308. In what book can you read about curse scars?

309. Who wrote 'Curses and Counter Curses'?

310. Who wrote the Dream Oracle?

# The Wizarding World – Part 2

311. How old are witches and wizards when they come of age?

312. What are the four different types of blood purity?

313. What is the main lift at the Ministry of Magic disguised as?

314. What are dark wizard catchers called?

315. What is the name of the place in London where witches and wizards go to shop?

316. Which object is used to transport wizards from one place to another at an arranged time?

317. How long ago was the Triwizard Tournament started?

318. How many people have survived the Avada Kedavra curse?

319. What is the address of Sirius' house?

320. What is the name of the department store which hides the main wizarding hospital?

# Professor Snape

321. What job are we told that Snape really wants?

322. Where did Professors Snape meet with Quirrell so they wouldn't be overheard?

323. What was James Potter's nickname for Snape?

324. Name the potion that Professor Snape threatens to use on Harry?

325. Where does Professor Snape live?

326. What did Mrs Malfoy want Snape to make?

327. What is the name of Snape's Mother?

328. And his Father?

329. Who went to visit Snape in his home?

330. Who does Snape make a monthly potion for whilst he is at Hogwarts?

# Beasts and Animals – Part 3

331. What kind of creature is Ronan?

332. Which Werewolf bit Remus Lupin?

333. The sound of which creature can kill a Basilisk?

334. Which two types of dragon are found in the British Isles?

335. What animal's blood should you feed (with brandy) to a Dragon?

336. Which creatures guard the lake in the cave where Harry finds a Horcrux with Dumbledore?

337. What is the name of Aunt Marge's dog?

338. How many giants does Hagrid think there are left?

339. And who is the Gurg?

340. What is the name of Hepzibah Smith's house elf?

# Quidditch – Part 3

341. Who was the last Gryffindor seeker to help win the Quidditch Cup?

342. What position did Lockhart say he played at Quidditch?

343. How many seconds does it take a Firebolt to accelerate from zero to 150 miles per hour?

344. What Quidditch team does Cho Chang support?

345. Who does Oliver Wood play for after leaving Hogwarts?

346. So who takes over from him at Griffindor?

347. Who captains the Holyhead Harpies?

348. How many years had it been since Britain last hosted the Quidditch World Cup?

349. What colour was the dark mark skull in the sky when Britain did host it after all that time?

350. And which house elf did Harry meet there?

# Other Characters – Part 3

351. Who were Sirius Black's parents?

352. Who is linked to both Hogwarts staff and the hospital?

353. What did Apollyon Pringle do at Hogwarts when Mrs Weasley was a student there?

354. Who were the first two death eaters to make it to the top of the Astronomy Tower after Draco?

355. Who liked being burned at the stake so much she allowed it to happen forty-seven times?

356. Who does Harry ask the minister to release from prison?

357. What is Neville's Great Uncle called?

358. What is Mrs Figg's first name?

359. Whose father was an Auror called Frank?

360. Who is Sirius's great-great-grandfather?

# Draco Malfoy and Friends

361. What did Malfoy take that belonged to Neville in book 1?

362. What are the first names of Crabbe and Goyle?

363. What offensive term did Malfoy first call Hermione in their second year?

364. Which shop does Draco attend in Knockturn Alley?

365. Who does Harry ask to watch Malfoy together?

366. How are Crabbe and Goyle disguised when on look out?

367. Who did Draco take to the Yule Ball?

368. To what size did Draco's nose swell during one of Professor Snape's Potions classes?

369. Who dressed up as dementors to scare Harry, along with Malfoy, Crabbe and Goyle?

370. Which spell did Professor Snape suggest Draco cast on Harry at the Duelling Club?

# The Weasley Family – Part 3

371. What does Ron vomit after casting a spell with his broken wand?

372. And what bit of 'specialist equipment' is given to him to help recover?

373. What are George and Fred's fireworks called?

374. What present did Fred and George try to send to Harry when he was in the hospital wing?

375. What did Bill develop a liking for after being bitten by a werewolf?

376. Which Ministry department does Percy Weasley first work for?

377. What is the name of Percy's girlfriend?

378. Who accompanies Percy to the Weasley's house on Christmas Day?

379. Who provided the twins with Venomous Tentacula seeds?

380. Who is Mrs Weasley's favourite singer?

# Spells and Potions – Part 3

381. What potion would Madam Pomfrey use to help cure colds?

382. What is it called when you leave half of yourself behind when apparating?

383. What potion do Asphodel & Wormwood make?

384. What is the spell to conjure the dark mark?

385. What simple spell would you use to start a fire?

386. What spell does Harry use to dangle Ron by his ankles?

387. What are the three things to think of when casting the apparition spell?

388. What spell is used to put out the fire at Hagrid's?

389. What ancient language do many spells rely on?

390. Which spell would you use to damage an opponent's eyesight?

# General Knowledge – Part 3

391. Where is the nearest portkey to the Weasleys' home?

392. Who is appointed as Buckbeak's Executioner?

393. How much did the Dursleys once give to Harry for his Christmas present?

394. How many Valentine's Day cards did Gilderoy Lockhart say he had received?

395. What length of parchment did Professor Binns ask for on the Medieval Assembly of European Wizards?

396. Which member of the order is a metamorphmagus?

397. Who was caught smuggling flying carpets into Britain?

398. When did The Griffindor Ghost die?

399. How many people could travel on Barty Crouch's Grandfather's Magic Carpet?

400. What are the four types of dragon used in the Triwizard Tournament?

# The Answers

# Harry – Part 1

1.   31st July

2.   4 Privet Drive, Little Whinging

3.   Hagrid

4.   A Lightning Bolt

5.   A Boa-Constrictor

6.   James

7.   Lily

8.   An Invisibility Cloak

9.   A Stag

10.   Cho Chan

# Hermione – Part 1

11.  Jean

12.  An Otter

13.  Viktor Krum

14.  A Time Turner

15.  Crookshanks

16.  It made her teeth grow

17.  Defence Against The Dark Arts

18.  Full Body Bind

19.  Dentists

20.  September

# Ron – Part 1

21.   Ginger

22.   Bilius

23.   Six

24.   A Howler

25.   A Pocket Sneakoscope

26.   Spellotape

27.   A Knight

28.   True

29.   A Spider

30.   Keeper

# Hogwarts – Part 1

# The Wizarding World – Part 1

41. Galleon, Knut and Sickle

42. The Dementors

43. St. Mungo's

44. A Plump, Blonde Witch

45. Mungo Bonham

46. The Wizengamot

47. The Daily Prophet

48. Hogsmeade

49. Butterbeers

50. Glass

# Beasts and Animals – Part 1

51.  The Philosophers Stone

52.  Music (specifically a Harp)

53.  Trevor

54.  Errol

55.  Buckbeak

56.  Witherwings

57.  A Boarhound

58.  Basilisk

59.  The Unicorn

60.  4

# Quidditch – Part 1

61.    Bludger, Quaffle and Golden Snitch

62.    150

63.    7

64.    Beater, Chaser, Keeper and Seeker

65.    Chudley Cannons

66.    A Nimbus 2000

67.    Oliver Wood

68.    Dobby

69.    Marcus Flint

70.    700

# Spells and Potions – Part 1

71.   Parseltongue

72.   Wingardium Leviosa

73.   Expelliarmus

74.   Three

75.   Avada Kedavra, Cruiciatus and Imperius

76.   Avada Kedavra - The Killing Curse

77.   Alohomora

78.   Lumos

79.   Riddikulus

80.   Expecto Patronum

# Other Characters – Part 1

81.   Professor Albus Dumbledore

82.   Death Eaters

83.   Madam Rosmerta

84.   Stan Shunpike

85.   Ernie Prang

86.   Nicolas Flamel

87.   Lee Jordan

88.   Dennis

89.   Regulus

90.   Cedric Diggory

# Books and the Like – Part 1

91. Red

92. The Daily Prophet

93. Hogwarts: A History

94. Chroniclus Punnet

95. Stroke its Spine

96. Which Broomstick

97. The Quibbler

98. Most Charming Smile

99. Bathilda Bagshot

100. The Half Blood Prince

# The Weasley Family – Part 1

101. Molly & Arthur

102. Ginny

103. Ford Anglia

104. The Burrow

105. Nine

106. Dean Thomas

107. Extendable Ears

108. Bill

109. Fleur Delacour

110. The Department of Mysteries

# Hogwarts Teachers – Part 1

111.  Professor Flitwick

112.  Professor McGonagall

113.  39 years

114.  A Tabby Cat

115.  Professor Binns

116.  He is a Werewolf

117.  Pomona

118.  Professor Dippet

119.  Professor Kettleburn

120.  He is a Squib

# General Knowledge – Part 1

121. Devil's Snare

122. Mermish

123. Stonewall High

124. He transformed into a Dog

125. Snuffles

126. Your Soul

127. Professor Umbridge

128. The Malfoys

129. Purple

130. Devon

# Shops

131. Ollivander's

132. Seven

133. Florean Fortescue

134. The Hogs Head and the Three Broomsticks

135. Weasleys Wizard Wheezes

136. 93 Diagon Alley

137. Robes

138. Honeydukes

139. The Magical Menagerie

140. Twelve Galleons

# Dumbledore

141. A Phoenix

142. The Sorting Hat and Godric Griffindor's Sword

143. It was the password to his office

144. Horcruxes

145. Six

146. In a Pensieve

147. Grindelwald

148. A Vulture

149. A Map of the London Underground

150. Twelve

# He Who Must Not Be Named

151. Lord Voldemort

152. Nagini

153. False

154. None

155. Thirteen and a half inches

156. The Hogwarts assistance fund

157. Borgin and Burke's

158. Ten Galleons

159. They are both Half-Bloods, they are both Orphans, and they both speak Parseltongue.

160. Little Hangleton

# Hagrid

161. A Wooden Flute

162. Keeper of Keys

163. In His Umbrella

164. Norbert

165. A Norwegian Ridgeback

166. The Monster Book of Monsters

167. Madame Maxine

168. His Mother

169. Fridwulfa

170. Grawp

# Harry – Part 2

# Hermione – Part 2

181. (The) Society for the Promotion of Elfish Welfare

182. Two Sickles

183. Hats and Socks for the House Elves

184. Dumbledore's Army

185. A Fake Galleon

186. Confundus

187. Cormac McLaggen

188. Professor Slughorn's

189. Charms

190. Ron

# Ron – Part 2

191. Viktor Krum

192. Willow with a Unicorn Tail Hair Core

193. Fourteen Inches

194. Sirius Black

195. Ginny

196. The Deluminator

197. Quidditch Keeper's Gloves

198. A Chocolate Cauldron

199. Lavender Brown

200. Bezoar

# Hogwarts – Part 2

201. Moaning Myrtle

202. Seven

203. The Fat Lady

204. Ordinary Wizarding Levels

205. The Room of Requirement

206. Three

207. Beauxbatons, Durmstrang and (of course) Hogwarts

208. Seventeen

209. A Whomping Willow

210. The Philosopher's Stone

# Beasts and Animals – Part 2

211. A Troll

212. A Snowy Owl

213. An Acromantula

214. Hagrid, Harry and Professor Slughorn

215. Acromantula Venom

216. The Kitchens at Hogwarts

217. Firenze

218. A Dog

219. Kreacher

220. A Spider

# Quidditch – Part 2

221. Cho Chang

222. Seamus Finnegan

223. Peru

224. Bulgaria

225. Ireland

226. Hassan Mostafa

227. 10 Galleons

228. Mahogany

229. Professor Umbridge

230. A Firebolt

# Spells and Potions – Part 2

# Other Characters – Part 2

241. A Beetle

242. Gabrielle

243. Remus Lupin

244. Xenophilius Lovegood

245. Tom

246. His Deathday Party

247. Hufflepuff

248. Bellatrix and Narcissa

249. Rufus Scrimgeour

250. Katie Bell

# The Weasley Family – Part 2

251.  The Marauder's Map

252.  Mollywobbles

253.  Fifty

254.  Onion Soup

255.  Barty Crouch

256.  Weatherby

257.  Twelve

258.  Hermes

259.  The Misuse of Muggle Artefacts Office

260.  One

# The Dursleys

261. Grunnings

262. Thirty-Six

263. Big D

264. Dudders

265. St. Brutus's Secure Centre for Incurably Criminal Boys

266. Twelve

267. The Accidental Magic Reversal Department

268. Red

269. Uncle Vernon

270. The Rail View Hotel

# Harry – Part 3

271. Wormtail / Peter Pettigrew

272. Occlumency

273. Willow

274. Buckbeak, His House and Kreacher

275. Luna Lovegood

276. Knockturn Alley

277. Draco Malfoy

278. Moaning Myrtle

279. Magnolia Crescent

280. Neville Longbottom

# Hogwarts Teachers – Part 2

281. Filius

282. An Examiner

283. Horace Slughorn

284. Hagrid

285. Firenze

286. Poppy

287. Gilderoy Lockhart

288. Professor Sprout

289. Astronomy

290. Professors Dumbledore and McGonagall

# General Knowledge – Part 2

291. Nastily Exhausting Wizarding Tests

292. The Shrieking Shack

293. Neville Longbottom

294. Remus Lupin, Peter Pettigrew, Sirius Black and James Potter

295. Kingsley Shacklebolt

296. Buckbeak

297. Fleur Delacour

298. 713

299. Sir Nicholas de Mimsy-Porpington

300. Forty-five

# Books and the Like – Part 2

301. The Tales of Beedle the Bard

302. Seven Hundred

303. A Belt

304. Roonil Wazlib

305. Libatius Borage

306. Eldred Worple

307. In Limericks

308. Common Magical Ailments and Afflictions

309. Vindictus Viridian

310. Inigo Imago

# The Wizarding World – Part 2

# Professor Snape

321. Defence Against the Dark Arts Teacher

322. The Forbidden Forest

323. Snivellus

324. Veritaserum

325. Spinner's End

326. An Unbreakable Vow

327. Eileen Prince

328. Tobias Snape

329. Bellatrix LeStrange and Narcissa Malfoy

330. Professor Lupin

# Beasts and Animals – Part 3

331. A Centaur

332. Fenrir Greyback

333. A Rooster

334. The Common Welsh Green and The Hebridean Black

335. Chicken

336. Inferi

337. Ripper

338. Eighty

339. The Chief of the Giants

340. Hokey

# Quidditch – Part 3

341. Charlie Weasley

342. Seeker

343. Ten

344. The Tutshill Tornados

345. Puddlemere United

346. Angelina Johnson

347. Gwenog Jones

348. Thirty Years

349. Emerald Green

350. Winky

# Other Characters – Part 3

351. Orion and Walburga

352. Dilys Derwent

353. He was the caretaker

354. Alecto and Amycus

355. Wendelin the Weird

356. Stan Shunpike

357. Algie

358. Arabella

359. Neville Longbottom

360. Phineas Nigellus

# Draco Malfoy and Friends

361. A Remembrall

362. Vincent and Gregory

363. Mudblood

364. Borgin and Burke's

365. Kreacher and Dobby

366. As Girls

367. Pansy Parkinson

368. A Melon

369. Marcus Flint

370. Serpensortia

# The Weasley Family – Part 3

371.  Slugs

372.  A Bucket

373.  Weasleys' Wildfire Whiz-Bangs

374.  A Toilet Seat

375.  Rare Steak

376.  The Department of International Magical Co-operation

377.  Penelope Clearwater

378.  Rufus Scrimgeour

379.  Mundungus Fletcher

380.  Celestina Warbeck

# Spells and Potions – Part 3

381.  Pepperup Potion

382.  To Splinch

383.  A Draught of Living Death

384.  Morsmordre

385.  Incendio

386.  Levicorpus

387.  Destination, Determination and Deliberation

388.  Aguamenti

389.  Latin

390.  Conjunctivitis

# General Knowledge – Part 3

391. Stoatshead Hill

392. Walden MacNair

393. Fifty Pence

394. Forty-six

395. Three Feet

396. Nymphadora Tonks

397. Ali Bashir

398. The 31st October 1492

399. Twelve

400. The Chinese Fireball, The Hungarian Horntail, The Swedish Short-Snout and The Welsh Green

# Also Available

From Andrews UK

Colin the Librarian

by Merv Lambert

ISBN: 978-1-78166-243-4

Colin the Librarian is an unremarkable little man, who one day at work finds a very rare, very unusual book. It does not belong to the library. On opening it he sees the title 'Colin's Book' and inside it is a beautiful blue bookmark with a red phoenix on it. The bookmark gives him extraordinary strength and resolve and leads him and his little dog Sammy into many exciting adventures both in the past and present...

# Excerpt from Colin the Librarian

Colin was an unremarkable little man, who worked in the library.

It was Tuesday morning and his least favourite person had just walked in.

"Oh, horror, horror!" he thought. Mrs. Biggle *was* big. She was always very bad tempered and unpleasant with everyone, including her husband and her children, but especially to her husband and Colin. Perhaps it was because Colin, being small, reminded her of her husband. She came striding into the library carrying two large shopping bags. Out of the first she took two DVDs and threw them rudely on the counter. Out of the second she took two books, which she also threw rudely on the counter. Colin picked up the two DVDs, 'The Black Mask of Castle Zorn' and 'The Luvvy Duvvy Wuvvies on Holiday'. "Ugh!" he shuddered. He thought the Black Mask was probably for Mr. Biggle and the children. The second was certainly Mrs. Biggle's choice. She was always taking out for herself what Colin thought were horrible yukky books. Colin never read them. He didn't think Mr. Biggle read very much. Quickly he passed the DVDs and books over the scanner.

"Late again, Mrs. Biggle. These are all overdue," he said. "The fine is £4"

"No! I'm not paying any fine!" shouted Mrs. Biggle. "You must have stamped the wrong date on them."

"No, no, no," replied Colin wearily. He knew Mrs. Biggle was always like this. She always got her own way, as the chief librarian Mr. Jellysox lived in the same street and was afraid of her.

"I want to see the manager!" bellowed Mrs. Biggle.

"You mean you want to see the chief librarian," said Colin.

Forewarned by Mrs. Biggle's shouting, Mr. Jellysox appeared from his office and approached nervously. He was a quite tall but tubby man. He always wore a yellow waistcoat and ghastly ties with colours that clashed horribly with it. Today's was a sickly lime green. He was also wearing bright yellow socks. His little eyes hid behind pebble glasses.

"Er, good morning, Mrs. Biggle," he said, wringing his hands anxiously. He knew what was coming. This had happened before.

Mrs. Biggle did not bother to say "Good morning". She glared at Mr. Jellysox, who seemed to wobble in fright. This was because he really was wobbling in fright.

"Would you like to come and sit in my office, Mrs. Biggle?" he said.

Mrs. Biggle took no notice of what he said. Instead she pointed at Colin and started shouting again.

"How dare this idiot say that my library books and DVDs are overdue!"

"I'm not an idiot...," Colin started to speak, but was interrupted by Mrs. Biggle.

"He *always* stamps the wrong date on them!"

"But...but..." stammered Mr. Jellysox.

"He does it on *purpose!*" roared Mrs. Biggle.

"No, no, I..." said Colin.

"No, no, he..." said Mr. Jellysox.

"Oh, yes he does!" shouted Mrs. Biggle, interrupting them both.

Since Mrs. Biggle refused to listen to anything they said, Colin grew more and more angry, but Mr. Jellysox grew more and more worried and terrified. Besides, she lived on the same street as him and could be a most annoying neighbour.

"Oh dear! Oh dear!" sighed Mr. Jellysox in dismay.

"Oh no! Oh no!" thought Colin. "Not again!" He knew that Mr. Jellysox would give in. Mr. Jellysox gave in. Colin knew exactly what Mr. Jellysox would say. He had said these words so often before.

"All right, Mrs. Biggle. You don't have to pay any fines. Colin, go and stamp today's date on the books and DVDs Mrs. Biggle has just brought in."

Colin was furious. He turned on his heel and went to do what his boss, Jellysox, had just told him to do.

Ten minutes later Mrs. Biggle walked out of the library, carrying two new books and two new DVDs. She had not handed over the money. Once again she had won. Mr. Jellysox slunk back,exhausted and ashamed, into his office.

Colin loved his job and shortly afterwards, as he was walking round among the bookshelves, he saw an old book that he had not noticed before. He put out his hand to take it. It had a dark leather cover and it felt warm to the touch. The faded gold letters on the front were not easy to read. Colin opened the book and read the title inside - 'Colin's Book'. He could hardly believe his eyes. There seemed to be lots of interesting and exciting things in it. Then his fingers touched something hidden in the pages. It looked like an ancient bookmark also made of leather and with a beautiful bird on it. Colin recognised it. It was a phoenix. The bookmark was dark blue but the feathers of the phoenix glowed red. Colin gently stroked them and he sensed a warm glow. He felt very calm and confident. It was almost as if the book were speaking to him aloud, saying, "You are my rightful owner. You always try to do the right thing." Colin, bewildered, shook his head. He noticed that there was no card inside the book cover for stamping the date for it to be returned. It did not belong to the library then. The book was telling him it belonged to him. Thoughtfully Colin carried the volume back to his desk and slid it into the pocket of his overcoat.

His good mood lasted all day. Finally, when it was time to go home, he tucked the bookmark into the top pocket of his jacket and put on the overcoat with the book still inside it. He began to walk home.

He had just got to Bluebottle Lane, where the Biggles and Mr. Jellysox lived, when he heard some shouting and snarling. He saw a very large boy dragging a very small dog on a lead along the pavement. The little dog was obviously afraid and did not want to go with him. The shouting and the snarling were coming from the boy.

"Come on!" the boy shouted and aimed a kick at the dog. "I hate having to take a stupid little animal like you for walks!"

Without thinking about it, Colin dashed forward. The bookmark seemed to be glowing more warmly in his pocket.

"Stop that!" he yelled.

The boy looked up, startled.

"Mind your own business!" he snarled. "Clear off, Shorty!" (Only those were not his exact words.)

"That's no way to treat a little dog!" said Colin, ignoring the boy's raised fist.

"I said, 'Clear off'!" shouted the boy. (Again that is not exactly what he said.)

Suddenly Colin knew just what to do. He snatched the dog's lead from the boy's hand and grabbed him by the front of his shirt.

"Listen," he said through gritted teeth. "Animals are supposed to be dumb. You are worse. You really *are* dumb. Understand? By dumb I mean stupid. You're a really dumb dumbo."

The boy had never met anyone with such a strong grip. The next moment, still grasping him by his shirt, Colin with one hand had lifted him off his feet and, whirling him round above his head, had thrown him through the thick hedge by the side of the road.

"Aaah! Ow!" howled the boy. Sharp twigs stuck out from him everywhere. He looked like a creature grown from a hedge.

"Hello, Twiggy!" called one of a group of older boys from his school, who happened to be passing by.

"I'll take the dog and look after him properly," said Colin, and set off down the street with it trotting happily beside him.

"Urgh! Ug! Grook!" The boy tried to say something, but had to remove a large twig from his mouth first. Finally he wailed, "Just you wait! I'll get the police on you!"

Colin took no notice. The bookmark felt nice and warm in his pocket.

Later that evening Colin had just given the little dog his first meal at his house, when there was a knock at the front door. He opened it. A large policeman stood there next to an equally large woman. It was Mrs. Biggle.

"Evening, sir," said the policeman. I'm Police Constable Wright."

Mrs. Biggle said nothing. She just did her usual thing. She glared angrily at Colin.

"Well, officer, what do you want?" asked Colin.

The policeman shuffled his feet uncomfortably. "Well, sir, do you own a dog?"

"Yes, as a matter of fact I do."

"This lady says that you have stolen *her* dog. May I see your dog, sir?"

"Yes, of course. Come in. Come in."

The policeman stepped into the house and followed Colin into the kitchen. Mrs. Biggle hurried in too.

"That's him! That's my Boggle!" she cried, pointing at the dog. The little animal, obviously frightened, had run to hide behind Colin.

"Is it?" asked the policeman.

Colin had already decided what was the right thing to say. The bookmark seemed to glow warm in his pocket. There was no way that he would let the little dog go back to a horrible family, who would mistreat it, and although it was not the truth, what he said next was the right thing.

"No, no, this isn't Boggle Biggle. It's Sammy. Here, boy." Kneeling down he coaxed the small dog to come to him. He stroked it. It looked up at him lovingly.

"Come here, Boggle!" snapped Mrs. Biggle, stepping angrily towards the dog and into a little puddle it had just made on the floor. The dog hid, whimpering, behind Colin, who said, "Well, officer, who do *you* think is the owner?"

"Let me look at his collar," said P.C. Wright. "Well, it's got his name Sammy and this address," he continued.

Colin had really been quite clever, for he had kept the collar worn by his other dog, which had died some years ago.

"Hmm." P.C. Wright also thought he knew what to do. He noticed that Colin had a certain sharp, steely way of looking at him. Colin was willing him to make the right decision. He made the P.C. Wright decision, and turning to Mrs. Biggle, he said, "It seems clear to me that Sammy belongs here. "As there is no evidence that the dog is yours, I feel sure it's a case of mistaken identity. If you want to take this further, madam, you could take the matter to court, but I'm not certain you would win, and it could cost you a lot of money."

"But,...but...," stammered Mrs. Biggle, who was used to getting her own way always.

"No buts, madam," continued P.C. Wright. "I'm telling you it must be a case of mistaken identity."

"But this man threw our Bradley through a hedge this afternoon!"

Looking at Colin, the policeman shook his head.

"No, I don't think so. Bradley is a big lad and this gentleman does not really look as if he could do that.

We're going now, madam." He shook hands with Colin. "Thank you for your time, sir," he said, and he almost pushed the angry Mrs. Biggle out of the house. Sammy yapped happily and ran to Colin.

The next morning Colin was again working in the library. The bookmark was still tucked in his pocket. It felt warm. He felt confident. Suddenly Mrs. Biggle stormed through the front door, dragging her husband behind her. He was a small, worried-looking man with a little toothbrush moustache.

"There he is!" she shouted, pointing at Colin. "Do something, Biggle!"

Mr. Biggle shrugged his shoulders helplessly and said nothing.

"Ah, Mrs. Biggle, just the person I wanted to see," smiled Colin. "Thank you for coming in so soon. I have spoken to Mr. Jellysox and persuaded him that you really *should* pay the fines you owe the library. Four pounds please." And he held out his hand. Mrs. Biggle was about to hit it with her umbrella, when she noticed a certain steely look in Colin's eyes. She froze.

The bookmark was still giving off a warm glow in Colin's pocket. "Of course, if you pay this time, we'll be prepared to forget all the others you have not paid, but in future you will not bully anyone here. Is that clear?"

Pierced by Colin's firm gaze, Mrs. Biggle was already reaching into her purse. She put four one pound coins down on the counter, turned and stomped out. Her husband, amazed, winked at Colin and gave him a thumbs-up sign, as he left.

Already Colin was thinking that he needed to begin reading his new old book. He had a strange feeling that something exciting was just starting. The phoenix bookmark glowed and pulsed in his pocket, as if agreeing with him.

Lightning Source UK Ltd.
Milton Keynes UK
UKOW051853120413

209158UK00009B/55/P